ANN ANDERSON

FEARLESS AND FIERCE

DYNAMIC PARADIGM MANAGEMENT

authorHOUSE®

AuthorHouse™
1663 Liberty Drive
Bloomington, IN 47403
www.authorhouse.com
Phone: 1 (800) 839-8640

Published by AuthorHouse 01/26/2019

ISBN: 978-1-5462-7691-3 (sc)
ISBN: 978-1-5462-7759-0 (e)

Print information available on the last page.

FOREWORD

Plan it for the future. I was inspired to write a book that changes people's habits because I know that we are all inspired by our family and our peers. Through all of my life coaching and research I discovered that a lot of our habits come from not just our family and not just our peers but some come from a far deeper genealogy. Some of it is good and some of it is not so good. Everyone needs to have a T Bar scale to evaluate why they do things and what people like about themselves and what they like about themselves and what they don't like about themselves and then evaluate the ways to change those values into positive future prosperous goals.

I was called to help a friend who was in prison in helping them change their values from a white collar crime to help stay out of prison. That is when I started writing this book Paradigm Life Management. I too was a victim of these blue white collar crimes that led me to further evaluate the importance of this book to be a part of every court system and prison study.

Not Everyone likes where they are at at this moment and sometimes it doesn't need to be just people in prison sometimes we just have people with daily habits that we want to change. I call it breaking the chains or the mold from our genetic background and our peers and our family. It doesn't mean that we don't love our family and our peers it just means that maybe we need to break away from that to become the real person that is in our brain and in our heart to become. It also means learning to love yourself and forgiving yourself first and forgiving your enemies for they know not what they do have done. Sometimes I call it," you have to consider the source."

If you don't like where you come from or you don't like what you see begin with yourself and make the changes there first, then learn to forgive those you can't change or haven't bothered to change. They don't see the fault and sometimes we don't even recognize the fault in our own self. When you put the faults into a perspective where they come from, then you can learn to begin to change who you are or who you were. Now you can love yourself forgive yourself and forgive your enemies. All of this has to come from wanting to change. Identifying the steps that it takes to change habits. Infuse all of your learning and your past experiences as past experiences. Learn to develop new techniques and ways to cope and accomplish what you want out of life. Any and all changes are up to you how you live your life and what's your plans and dreams and goals are for the future.

It is important to want to change for the future to become a better person to become a better you. No one can make you change but you and the steps you take to improve. I hope you make it a positive change and I hope you make a better future for yourself. I hope this book will help you to become a kinder more forgiving and loving respectable person to give back to the universe the same kind of love and respect and teaching others to love them and forgive their enemies as well as themselves.

I have also learned that sometimes the things that we hate is because their habits that we are own selves have in our background by someone that has influenced us. I believe we can learn to love what we hate by accepting the source. Usually when we hate something it is a flaw in our own background. By learning to accept the flaws you can learn to love what you hate making that a positive rather than a negative in your personality. You can say I hate criminals but what you're really saying is that you hate when people provoked crime against you. That's okay because you don't have to love criminals and you don't have to love the crime that they commit against you. what I'm saying is it is a challenge to turn every negative into a positive. When you create a positive atmosphere it calms the nervous system.

I believe in karma when you put Good Karma out you get good karma back. Be careful of what you say because you are what you say it's like the law of attraction we become Who We Are by what we say and by what we do in our actions. Be good to yourself and to others it creates good Harmony and a positive atmosphere for everyone. Treat people the way you would like to be treated.

My background in life experiences and life coaching and my many Life Experiences have led me to writing this book for everyone, even children to use as a guide to changing their life in a positive blessed Manor of well-being to spread through the universe to teach others as well as themselves.

CONTENTS

INTRODUCTION

Welcome to the dynamic paradigm management program workbook. Over the course of the next six weeks, you will learn new skills to help you define your goals and values that you want to attain in your lifetime, beginning now. You will learn to use these skills to help you in attaining these goals as well as being able to communicate the help you will need from others in attaining these goals. You will identify your goals by categories, that being, short term, medium term and long term goals, making sure that all of these goals are in balance. Then you will develop an action plan that is realistic, helping you to attain your goals.

You will learn about values and how they are related to goals and then you will align your personal values to your goals. You will look at all of your habits, both good and bad. Then see how you can change your bad habits to good habits that you will follow now and in the future.

You will be asked to identify your personality or what you believe is your personality. Then review the descriptions and see if they are close to being correct.

Other topics to be covered include, communication skills, negotiation skills and time management.

You will be asked over the course of the next six weeks if you are willing and able to devote your energy into this program and an action plan. Just working through this workbook will take up a great deal of time and energy. When we finish the sixth week you will then be on your own to finish where we leave off.

You have made the first step in changing your paradigm and attaining your goals. This manual will help you to achieve a better understanding of your goals and values and planning to attain them. The bottom line is that this program is totally up to you. It will only work if you make it work. This workbook is your key to attaining your goals, now and in the future. Use it to the fullest to achieve the most. All that we ask of you is the desire to complete this program and attain your goals.

Oh, by the way in case you are wondering about how to begin in attaining your goals. Look at it this way, you already started by being here. Imagine you already completed goal <u>number one.</u> <u>Helping you!</u>

<u>YOUR</u> <u>GOALS</u> <u>ARE</u> <u>ATTAINABLE</u>!

The <u>Dynamic Paradigm Management Program</u> you are about to begin was developed and written while I was incarcerated at a Federal Prison. IT was written over the course of six month, using knowledge attained one twenty years, both working on the outside as will as working while incarcerated. The material enclosed is comprised of program that I have been involved with, either as a teacher as student. Together as they are presented here, I know from personal experience, this works. I was given the opportunity to teach their program at the institution.

This program is not just about setting and attaining goals. It is about communication, life, and accomplishing what you set out to do. It is about feeling good about what you have accomplishing for yourself and for others. It is about attaining whatever you set your sights on.

The program is separated into six sessions. Each session built upon the last. For the program to be beneficial, you need to complete each session. Starting this program and quitting at the end of session three or four, or as not following your destiny after the program is finished, will in no way help you to attain your goals. <u>You need it all!</u>

What inspired me to develop and write this program was my own inability since my incarceration to set my sight on realistic goals, and like concern for fellow inmates. So a calling was to put faith to me by me and my fellow inmates Use my experience in the outside world and the world of incarceration and develop a program to help us.

After developing the program and the completion of writing the workbook, I followed the course daily as advised, reading and re-rereading all our answers to the questions asked. Being able to analyze and understand your own answers. Many times setting with each other as a support group, to discuss our answers and questions. While using the program daily with the help of the others, I was able to refine the program to its present stage, where we would get the most use out of the program. The purpose was to give the "you" the student, as well as future instructors a positive and practiced way to attain your goals. I have seen first hand how this program, not only changed their life, but the lives of those who are around them. The program is designed to not only show you, but also to show others that you can be responsible and trusting member of your family and society as well as being a pastime influence on both. This program is not easy. Trust me. You will find that you will need the help and support of the others to get through it, whether they are friends or family and friends on the outside. You will be asked questions that are thought provoking, personal, that will require deep thought and discussion. Here again, you will need the help of family and friends to get to the root of the answer. It is all part of the strategy of the program. Just remember that that is what the program is about. This is to force you to look deeply inside yourself and your past as well as your hereditary past or genealogical past histories, to understand why you are the way you are and if you do not like what is there, then an opportunity of chance to change by setting goals. Ask yourself the questions posed to you and answer them honestly. It is designed to force you to look at your life and how it has affected you and your family and friends. Make you think how you could be a better 'you' and change your feelings to better your life.

First, you have to begin with yourself. You need to reach deep inside your mind, heart, and soul, then devote all that energy to complete this program. Without that devotion and hard work, this program will be of little help to you. This program and its success are completely up to you. Make use of what you will.

Let us be honest at this point, this program will not guarantee your future. This is up to you to guarantee your own future. This program can only help you to define, desire, and devise a way of making you a better person with goals to make it happen. Again, there are no guarantees. It is in your hands. This is just a guide to get you started and help you to follow through on your design of life by understanding your past and your heredities past. Learning to forgive, forget, and make new plans of how to change or correct the situations of your past. This now becomes your Bible of life.

Keep this book handy, once you have completed the program, to keep your goals and revise as necessary. Reference your goals whenever you get into a rut. Follow your dreams, plans, and goals. Remember what you start now is your future; do not let it slip away. Now is the time to make the best use of this program and its value. What you thought you could not achieve may be achievable. Look deep into every thought and idea. No thoughts or ideas are stupid or unreal they just need to be defined and worked out to a logical conclusion.

I have seen this program work for others as well as myself. I have seen it work on the outside for family members and friends. Business men and women have used it to organize their lives as well as homemakers who are looking to change their life. People just like you and me who want to define and attain their goals. Do not sit there and think it will not work, because if you think it will not work – it will not. You are what you choose to be now and in the future. Because you are incarcerated, this is actually an ideal time to start changing your thought pattern and goals. It is the best time to put all your thoughts and goals down in written form. Work them out and come to a conclusion and a plan. What the heck, you have the time to put them into a positive venture.

Remember to keep your ideas, goals, and values positive. Nothing negative is ever accomplished for the good of our surroundings. Building a positive minds and structure your goals accordingly will accomplish successful futures. <u>Look at where you are now with the desire to better yourself for your future.</u>

I have used this program to a positive end. I did not just sit down and write this program from my head. I put every toll in this booklet to work. I followed it just as I would a business plan as my instruction plan. It became my philosophy of life. The result was finding out that being dysfunctional in my own family, I was able to achieve my goals. No matter what the obstacles were, I had reason to follow my plan. It has worked for me. I hope you will find the key to make it work for you.

If during the course of this program, you have question in regards to my use of the program, do not hesitate to ask questions. Never let a question go unanswered especially when it pertains to your future. That is what we are here for, to prepare you for your future. To prepare you for success and help you get where you would like to be in your life. I will answer your questions to the best of my ability. I will answer them honestly and let you know my feelings and thoughts on how this program has helped me to see a future.

Now there is one last point to be made. How many times have you asked yourself, will I ever find the right person to love? I am sure that with me it happens often. Using this program also can help you in ways you never thought possible. I never lost hope in my thoughts about that. I always set that as a goal. I never gave up on it.

I wish you the greatest success and happiness in finding your goals. REMEMBER THAT IT IS UP TO YOU FOR THE GOODS TO COME OUT OF THIS COURSE.
IT IS ALL-GOOD!

What does an effective leader look like?

1. Authenticity. 2. Self-expression. 3. Value creation.

1. Link between inner and outer person truly authentic leaders are:
   1. Open both to their gifts and to their undeveloped qualities.
   2. People, who understand who they are, tend to have more powerful voice.

Leadership comes from one of two places
        Persona or character.
Persona is the coping part of our personality
        Mark that we create to protect ourselves from external stress and internal fear.
Character, is the essence of who we are
        It goes beyond what we do.

Self-expression: it goes beyond telling the truth
        It demonstrates a total sequence between who you are and what you do and say
Value creation: leaders create value through relationships.
    Admitting that you do not have all the answers is a big part of building good relationships. This is a big part of getting good results.

    Do you know yourself?
    Get in the habit of asking you two critical questions.
        1. Why do I pursue the work and the life that I have?
        2. What do I act like during the most fulfilling times of my life?

Do you know how to listen and to hear?
Do you hear others fears? Aspirations?
    When you hear at the deeper level, you will get information from people that you need. People will know you can understand them and they will eagerly count on you to listen to their stories.
What is your appreciation ratio?
    Appreciation is truly value creation
    Actually—it energizes people, and it makes them want to exceed their goals and perceived limits.

THREE REASONS OF FAILURE

1. Being able to adapt during transitions
   Resistant to change
   Cannot or will not behavior.
2. Difficult to work with.
   Resistant and manipulative and overly critical
   Insensitive to learning and listening.
3. Fail to lead in a team centered way?
   Being assertive and taking initiative can put people on the fast track early on. But those same tracts can stymie people when they reach the executive levels where teamwork is vital. Everyone is a part of the team.

I want you to imagine yourself in a quiet peaceful place. Relax a few moments then imagine you are surrounded by idols or successful people. Who do you see? Now pick the ones you think will make a difference in your life. Who are they? Can you imagine a table or Round table discussion with them? Imagine yourself to be perfect or in a higher Place that would control your decisions. You are the head of the round table to discuss how to be successful or a better person than you have been in your life. These people know all the answers you are looking for. Now you get to ask them how to be a better person. You can have your higher self as a person at your round table. This person is Angelic to you. This person is the one who will save you from sin and wrong decisions. You could have God at your round table…or Jesus Christ or Mohammed. It does not matter as long as you can clearly know what they will say or tell you when you need to make changes or decisions in your life. These people love you and care about you at your round table. They know all the right answers to your success or problems you encounter. Just close your eyes for 30 minutes and ask them all the questions you need and let them answer in your imaginary way that you think they would talk to you as a friend and successful business partner. Or take all the time you need to meditate with your round table partners.

Do this every day or whenever you need help or advice to make important decisions. Think of the outcome and the effects it will have on you and others around you. Think of ways to make better decisions and successful relationships with the people you need to be around to succeed. Help others to achieve their dreams as well. Work on yourself first and the rest will follow. Keep doing this daily or weekly until you have a clear picture of your dreams and goals. Write them down and take action for planning how to achieve what you want and need to succeed. Chinese proverb says you must Wake up for your dreams to be a reality. You first need to love yourself and who you are yet to become. Then forgive yourself for not being the person you have always wanted to be. Then take all the blame and place it on yourself. You are the only one responsible for making decisions. From now on you are the Master of your Future. It is up to you. Now learn to forgive everyone in your past for your decisions or problems you encountered. Meet the new YOU.

This book is interactive and requires the reader's participation. Use the book as an outline. Begin with a personal notebook that you write in your own story of your life. Begin with your ancestors and your most influential history of your life. This book is in sessions, preferably weekly interactions. Take your time in being honest with yourself. Use a "T" scale of positives and negatives and why? You think you are the way you are.

Each week follow the sessions if you feel you are ready to move on to the next session You may need to hire a life coach to keep you accountable or find an accountability friend to help you. Change what you need to and keep on improving until you change what you want to change. Some things are easy and some take time. Keep a record of tasks to keep you motivated. If you are not self-motivated you may need to have a friend or a coach keep you going. Some goals are good with 30 days some take 60-90 days to implement. The habits you want to change. Be consistent with your tasks and goals. Somethings will remain in the previous session until that goal is achieved while other task can move on to the next session. You are in control of writing and re-writing your life. You are the main actor, director and editor of your life. In the end it becomes you the imaginable person you want to be. There is no right or wrong sequences. Only progression steps to move forward and not backwards. Steps are up and down. With small landings to rest until you reach the top. …Now, go with the sessions even if it takes 20 years to complete. You get to write and plan with actions of your life movie before your eyes and on the way to being fearless and fierce!

SESSION I

The happiest people in the world do not
Necessarily have the best of everything.
They just make the best of everything.

In this session you are asked to write down your goals for now and in the future as you have defined them. If you have a problem answering these questions, do not get discouraged. This is the beginning. The purpose is to see if you have ever really thought about your goals and how you will achieve them.

You may find it tough to answer these questions without spending a great deal o time looking into yourself. This is not the session for that. You are just looking to see where you are at this very moment. Think of this as a check sheet for the future. Once you answer these questions, you will be asked to review them in the future sessions to see if they still meet with your goals and values, after going through a few weeks of this program.

Do not let this session scare you. If you cannot answer a question, move on. The end of the program will answer all your questions.

You need to see---- you cannot punch at something
You must punch through it.

Write down goals you want to attain now, 1 year from now, 5 years from now, 10 years from and 20 years from now.

_____

_____

_____

_____

_____

_____

_____

_____

_____

_____

As you look at these goals, do you feel they are realistic and why? Make baby steps to climb to the top. Do not expect success in one day.

_____

_____

_____

_____

_____

_____

_____

_____

_____

_____

_____

To attain these goals answer the following questions:

A. What resources are needed? Study books or videos etc.

_____

_____

_____

_____

B. Can you begin working on your future goals now? If so what will you do to begin? Do you need grants or education or research more details

_____

_____

_____

C. Who will you need in the way of family and friends to help you attain these goals? Or what services are offered to help you get started?

_____

_____

_____

Do you have the time and energy to start and complete these goals? What do you need to begin? Where do you see yourself being financially able? What tools do you need to start?

_____

_____

_____

_____

Have you looked at the positives and negatives of your goals? If not do that now and list them as you see them at this time. Take a paper and draw a line down the middle for +and – then summarize here.

_____

_____

_____

_____

Have you looked at the positives and negatives of your goals? If not do that now and list them as you see them at this time. Do the same as above here.

_____

_____

_____

_____

Do your short term, medium term, and long term goals relate to each other?

     Yes

          Check one…..

_____ No

Do your goals relate to your values?

_____ Yes

          Check one….

_____ No

Do you know what your values are?

_____ yes

        Check one….

   no

If you answered no, use this space and try and define your values, as you believe they are. If you are unsure of the meaning of values look in the glossary for a definition: or do more research to get what you need to achieve your dreams and goals.

_____

_____

_____

_____

_____

If you answered no, use this space and try to define your values as you believe they are. If you are unsure of the meaning of values look in the glossary for a definition and research more to get the right answers to qualify your answers.

_____

_____

_____

_____

_____

If you answered yes, make a list of your values as you perceive them today and include a brief description of how they relate to your goals:

_____

_____

_____

_____

_____

_____

_____

_____

_____

_____

_____

Who were your idols as you were aging?

_____

_____

_____

_____

_____

_____

Why were they your idols?

_____

_____

_____

_____

What was the influence of any of these idols on your life, if any?

SESSION II

TO BREAK A BAD HABIT, DROP IT!

Session two is devoted to your personal life history. It is a time for reflective thinking, remembering the past to help in planning the future. You need to be as honest as you can in answering these questions. No one is going to see this section except for you or whoever you let see it. It is personal and confidential; but needed to help you in getting in touch with what you must do to attain your goals.

You may find questions that don't worry you, in some way all these questions relate to your future as well as your past. Give them a chance. Answer all the questions before judging them. Remember, this program is for you.

The questions as stated deal with very personal information to help planning goals. You need to look into yourself for the answers. You may not like some of the answers that you come up with, but if you are completely honest this session will help you in defining and attaining your goals and realizing your true values that you believe in.

This session is very important to the rest of this program. Do not just brush it off. It will not go away. It is always going to be part of your life. As bad as it may be, see if you can use some of the bad and turn it to good.

In this session you are asked to write down your goals for now and in the future as you have defined them. If you have a problem answering these questions, do not get discouraged. This is the beginning. The purpose is to see if you have ever really thought about your goals and how you will achieve them.

You may find it tough to answer these questions without spending a great deal of time looking into yourself. This is not the session for that. You are just looking to see where you are at this very moment. Think of this

as a check sheet for the future. Once you answer these questions you will be asked to review them in future sessions to see if they still meet with your goals and values after going through a few weeks of this program.

So, do not let this session scare you. If you cannot answer a question, move on. The end of this program will answer all your questions.

When and where were you born? _____

Does where you were born have any effect on your life decisions? If so Why?

How will you overcome that obstacle?

_____

Are you still living at home? _____

_____

How many brothers and or sisters do you have? _____

_____

_____

_____

_____

Do your family members have a good support system? _____

_____

_____

Do you have any fears holding you back? Fear is a liar cast all your fears into the fire.

_____

Are you happy with the support from your family members?

_____

_____

What can they do to help you better yourself?

_____

_____

What kind of habits or criminal activities were you involved in?

_____

_____

How will you change your habits to become a more likeable responsible you?

_____

_____

_____

_____

Do you know why you need to change and what do you expect to happen with your changes?

_____

_____

_____

Is there a support group that will help you? Will you get involved if there is?

_____

Is it a pattern of your hereditary background? Alternatively, peers, or friends?

_____

_____

At what age and who or what influenced you in this life?

_____

_____

_____

What obstacles are you encountering at this time?

_____

Will you do research and interact with someone to help you change or overcome problems?. Who will help you?

_____

_____

_____

_____

How do you believe you can overcome these obstacles? You must believe and trust in yourself to make good decisions. Go to your round table and get the help you need or research the problem on the internet and get help with a professional to get the direction or answers you need to make it work

_____

_____

What are your goals at this time? Sometimes we need to change our plans and goals. Be positive and Never give up. You are the keeper of your Dreams and Goals. Sometimes we need to replace ourselves with people who are more meaningful and helpful who are successful. We may even need to relocate. Make your goals fit your personality and skills. If you need more skills research and get the info or resources need to qualify your actions. Put your plans into actions to achieve desired results.

_____

_____

_____

_____

_____

_____

_____

_____

_____

_____

_____

_____

_____

_____

_____

Is your mother or father still part of your life? How do they control or support you in your decisions?

_____

How many brother or sisters do you have? Are they still part of your life? Do they have any control or effects on your decisions?

_____

_____

_____

Do you still rely on your mother, father or any other family members for moral and, or financial support? Give a brief description. Maybe it is the reverse, Do they rely on you?

_____

_____

_____

_____

Do you have family (wife and children or ex-wife) that still rely on you for support? Give a brief description. Or do you rely on them?

_____

_____

_____

Will you return to them or to a new location when you are released if that is the case? Make sure you surround yourself with successful people that support your decisions or help you make the right decisions.

_____

_____

_____

How many years have you been into bad habits or criminal activity?

_____

Have you ever been in jail prison or an institution that controlled you?

_____

Do you feel life is easier by letting the system control your life and freedom?

If yes, Why, and will you continue this behavior?

_____

_____

_____

For what reasons did you hurt anyone by your actions?

_____

_____

_____

_____

Do you deserve to be punished or rewarded for your actions?

It is time to reward yourself with a new you and new decision maker. Take actions to refresh your education or surroundings. Gain posture and become a likable, loveable, resourceful, knowledgeable and wise in making Great Decisions to improve and better serve yourself and others around you.

_____

_____

How long will it take to change your habits?
Do you desire better behaviors or habits to be a better person?

_____

Will you take action to change?

Have you ever been controlled by someone or something?

_____

For how long? _____ Who did you hurt if any? And Why?

_____

_____

_____

_____

This is you taking responsibility for your actions. You own it now it is time to forgive yourself and move forward with power and Fierce convictions to change for the love of yourself.

_____

_____

How did you hurt your victims or your family?

_____

_____

_____

Whom do you blame for your problems? And why are they to blame?

_____

_____

_____

_____

Do you think you deserve the punishment you got? _____
What did you deserve? How would life be if you took the actions needed to help yourself and the ones your hurt to make your life better? You may not be able to help the ones you hurt but if you could, what would you do? Life is very complicated because we can't control what others do only what I do. Meaning you are responsible for your actions. You own them. Why not go to your round table and use your wisdom to forgive yourself and love yourself. No matter what happens you need to have to power to be fearless and move on to better things that make you happy and do not hold you back.

_____

_____

Do you plan on continuing to punish them or do you want to forgive yourself and change to be a new person who will not continue this kind of activity in the future. _____

_____

_____

_____

_____

_____

_____

Will you forgive yourself and your friends and family that have influenced you to be the way you are? Even if they do not forgive you it is okay. At least you tried. You did not fail unless you let yourself fail. Look for the positive to improve your outcome no matter what. Choose to be happy and let them know

_____

_____

_____

_____

_____

_____

_____

Will you ever forgive and forget the past to become a better you?

_____

_____

_____

_____

Answer these questions when you understand yourself and can truly accept the past and forgive everyone including yourself. It has to be that you want to change. No one in this world can make you change. Change only comes from within. The desire to Succeed and become the person you idolize.

Think about your influences and your upbringing and your morals are they all out of balance? Think about your ancestor's that may have an influence on the way you are. If you get a chance to watch the movie "The "Secret" Laws of Attraction" you may find yourself wanting new friends and new goals. These are all possible scenarios of why we are the way we are.

At what age did you start and how were you influenced to get involved with habits that you would like to change? (Friends, family, etc.)?

_____

_____

_____

_____

_____

_____

_____

What obstacles did you encounter at the beginning of your life of crime?

_____

_____

_____

_____

_____

_____

_____

_____

_____

_____

_____

_____

How did you overcome these obstacles, or how do you plan to overcome in the future?

_____

_____

_____

_____

_____

_____

_____

_____

During this time what were your goals?

_____

_____

_____

_____

_____

_____

_____

_____

_____

_____

_____

Do you understand the difference between goals and values? If yes, explain your values as you understand them. If no, leave blank until discussed. During this time what were your values, as you understood them?

_____

_____

_____

_____

_____

_____

_____

_____

_____

Have you reached any milestones and goals in your life that you are proud of?

_____

_____

_____

_____

_____

_____

_____

_____

_____

_____

_____

_____

During this time, what were the milestones you reached?

_____

_____

_____

_____

_____

_____

_____

_____

_____

_____

_____

Who helped you to attain these goals and milestones?

_____

_____

_____

_____

_____

_____

_____

_____

_____

Who do you give credit for your awards or milestones?

_____

_____

_____

_____

_____

_____

_____

_____

_____

What did the people who helped you, bring into your life to help you attain these goals and milestones?

_____

_____

_____

What resources did you rely on to attain these milestones and goals? There is always room for improvement. What else can you do to make life better? What habits do you need to change to improve your quality of life or health status? What will make you a more likeable person? Self-evaluations are important for health and social involvement.

_____

_____

_____

_____

_____

_____

_____

_____

_____

_____

What resources did you rely on during this time to survive?

_____

_____

_____

_____

_____

_____

_____

_____

_____

What obstacles did you encounter and how did you overcome them?

_____

_____

_____

_____

_____

_____

_____

_____

What resources did you rely on and how much success did you achieve at gaining access to your intended victims?

_____

_____

_____

_____

_____

_____

How do you deal with others? Especially friends who sometimes turn against you? What do you kike about yourself and what do others like about you? Are you willing to work on Self-improvement to better love yourself. Sometimes this is the 1st step to all your goals. Health and beauty are also relevant to someone who wants social status or finding a partner. Again you are in control to improve all the way around. Take a paper and draw a line and put the positives on one side and the negatives on the other side then find the ones you want to change for the better of what you do and do not like about yourself

_____

_____

_____

_____

_____

_____

_____

_____

_____

_____

_____

_____

_____

_____

List your strengths and weakness as they relate to your life, your work, your family and friends?

_____

_____

_____

_____

_____

_____

_____

_____

_____

_____

_____
_____
_____
_____
_____

How much of your time and energy do you spend in the day for preparing for the future relating to your goals?

_____
_____
_____
_____
_____
_____
_____
_____

Do you believe you are ready for the future and what it holds?

Check one....... _____ yes _____ no
Do you know what it means to be co-dependent? Explain?

_____
_____
_____
_____
_____

Is there any one that you are co-dependant on to help you with your future? And why do you rely on them? _____

_____
_____
_____

Does this co-dependency help you or hinder you in your goal planning? And Why? _____

_____

_____

_____

_____

Can you ever break away form this co-dependency if it is in the way of your dreams? And WHY?

_____

_____

_____

_____

SESSION III

IF YOU REALLY AND TRULY WANT TO DO
SOMETHING, YOU WILL FIND A WAY. IF YOU
DON'T, YOU WILL FIND AN EXCUSE.

IN SESSION THREE, YOU ARE GOING TO WORK ON FIVE
SEPARATE TOPICS.

The first is being your life of crime and how it has affected you, your
family, and friends. Also, you will be asked to consider how your time
incarcerated has affected you, your family, and friends.

Next, you will be asked to list your good habits as well as your bad
habits. Briefly stating why you think they are good or bad, and then
seeing if there is a way to change your bad habits to good habits.

The third topic to be covered in this session is devoted to helping you
to identify your type of personality from the list provided. You may
not find what you believe to be your type, but there is a good selection
to choose from. If you don't feel you fit any of these personalities,
you are welcomed to decide on another that you feel fits you. The
personalities that have been chosen by us have clues along with them
to help you to make a change.

In the fifth part of our session, we will deal with values. What they
are, how they relate to your goals and their importance in attaining
your goals and staying on track with your action plan. Your will
review your goals from session one and then align your values that you
have written here with your goals and see if they still are in balance.

How have family and friends affected your life? _____
_____
_____
_____

_____

_____

How has your life and activities affected your family and friends

_____

_____

_____

_____

_____

_____

How has your life and activities affected your personality?

_____

_____

_____

_____

How has your life been affected by your bad habits or criminal life on the street or society?

_____

_____

_____

_____

_____

_____

_____

How has your habitual life orcriminal life on the street or society affected others?

_____

_____

_____

_____

_____

How has your time in jail affected your life?

_____

_____

_____

_____

_____

_____

_____

How has your time in jail affected the life of others?

_____

_____

_____

_____

_____

What do <u>you</u> have to do to change your old ways?

_____

_____

_____

_____

_____

_____

_____

List your **good** and **bad** habits and why you think they are:

<u>Good</u>   **<u>bad</u>**

_____	_____
_____	_____
_____	_____
_____	_____
_____	_____
_____	_____
_____	_____

_____ _____
_____ _____
_____ _____
_____ _____
_____ _____
_____ _____
_____ _____
_____ _____
_____ _____

List your **bad habits** and ways **you** can change them to have **good habits:**

_____
_____
_____
_____
_____
_____
_____
_____
_____
_____
_____
_____
_____
_____
_____
_____
_____
_____
_____
_____
_____

Do you feel **you** can change your **bad habits** to **good habits**?

Check one..._____yes _____no
Remember you are in control now. No one can control you. You are responsible for your actions. Make Great Choices. Your round table is only a meditation away.

_____

From the list of personality types below, choose the ones you feel best represent your true self. Before you look up there definitions, write why you feel this type of personality describes you. Then look at the definitions of these types of personalities at the end of this section and see if you still agree with you first choice. If not make your corrections now.

_____ **Dreamer** _____ **worrier** _____ **Defiler** _____ **crisis-maker**
_____ **perfectionists** _____**overdoes** _____**OTHER**

Use this space for your reasons why:

Now make a personal inventory of the following items:

A. **Knowledge skills (what you know):**

_____

_____

_____

_____

B. **Performance skills (what you can do):**

_____

_____

_____

_____

_____

_____

_____

_____

_____

C. **Personal attributes (what you value & how you act)**

_____

_____

_____

_____

_____

_____

D. **Environmental needs (where you are comfortable):**

_____

_____

_____

_____

_____

_____

_____

_____

_____

_____

E. Satisfaction (what you like):

_____

_____

_____

_____

_____

Before we continue, we will now take this time to work on and understand how your values relate to your goals and how they will help you to attain your goals. You need a strong desire for change and a commitment to understand your basic elements to succeed. The will power to achieve and the stamina to conquer your fears and turn them into strengths to accomplish your dreams is a main factor. Where does Religion fit into your life? Support Groups and clubs or Association that make your life improve are a benefit to network and realize we are all human to make mistakes and overcome problems and never has to be alone. Your goal may include others who have the same desires. It may be a relationship to improve or obtain a partnership for love or business. Whatever you do make good decisions. Remember not to control everyone around you. You can be an asset the others by letting them make decisions also. You can only control what you do. Be kind to others always make them feel important and welcome them and accept the way they are. You can love someone and not like them at the same time also vice versa you may not like someone's actions but learn to accept who they are. I may love you and not like your actions, so I may have to compromise and accept what you do as long as it does not interfere with my goals. In that case I may need to make some changes. Always be ready to accept or try to understand someone else's position. Don't make it your problem though. They have to own their own actions and be willing to change if it desires them to do so.

If not, no problem for you. You have enough of your own. If you do not like yourself then change. Go to your round table and meditate.

_____

_____

_____

_____

_____

_____

_____

_____

_____

_____

What are my values, (family, financial security, vacation, health, friends, etc.)?

_____

_____

_____

_____

_____

_____

_____

_____

_____

_____

Number your values in the order of importance to you: then create actions to obtain these goals. Build a dream board and make it fun. Include your partners and friends if you like.

_____

_____

For each value answer the following questions: Is it obtainable with my plans.

A. How important is this value to you now and in the future? Why?

_____

_____

_____

_____

_____

_____

_____

_____

B. How will it affect you and others in your life?

_____

_____

_____

_____

Do you believe that these values will change when you are released? Give reasons for both yes and no answers:

_____

_____

_____

_____

_____

_____

_____

SOME HELPFUL IDEAS IN SETTING GOALS

Is your goal realistic or a dream of what you would like to fall in your lap, but are not willing to work for? Many people think that they would like to buy a Rolls Royce, but are not willing to save or go out and earn the money needed to purchase this goal.

A reason for not accomplishing a goal is because it does not fit in with what you feel is most important to you. If you value education and your goal is to finish high school or college in the next few years, but your highest priority is working out in the gym everyday and it is taking up a great deal of your time so you are making excuses, you may want to redefine your time frame of accomplishing your goal of education, so that you won't be disappointed when you fail to reach your goal in the time frame you started with.

Is your goal specific enough so that you will know when you have achieved it? Is it achievable within a definite time frame that you can set for yourself and accomplish? Do you have access to the resources necessary to achieve it? Rather than saying that you want to "retire on a comfortable income", you may want to set a date for retirement and specify an amount of money that you know you can realistically earn and save to achieve your goal!

Now it is timed to see if your values match up to your goals. In the next session we will begin to identify your goals for year one and try to see where our values that we have described in this section fit in. Some of your values may be ties to longer term goals. This is the time to identify them and take the appropriate action.

DREAMERS

These procrastinators desperately want life to be easy and free from pain. They retreat from the real world and live in their heads, where everything is vague, nonthreatening and cozy. They cherish the notion that they are special that they don't have to play by the rules. This kind of "magical thinking" often leads to employment problems; spouses who tire of unkempt promises and the assuming of disguises as they flee collection agencies from state to state.

SOLUTION

If this sounds like you, you need to leave "peter pan" behind. Recognize the difference between "feeling good at the moment" (fantasizing, watching TV, buying stuff) and "feeling good about yourself" (the pleasure of accomplishment). Learning to use new software, increasing the amount of weight you are lifting, getting an education, etc. This won't be as much fun as watching basketball, but yields greater self-respect and confidence. You also need to ground yourself in the here and now. Lists are good for this. Write down what realistically be accomplished each day and the specific steps that must be taken to do it. Develop a passion for the "middle" stage of projects, that detail-rich area where you tend to check out.

WORRIERS

The worrier prizes security above all else and pays a steep prices for it. He has a narrow comfort zone and paralyzes himself with anxiety when faced by risk or change. They suffer from anticipation of negative hypothetical situations. "what if I can't" find a job?" "What if I don't like the job I have?" Worriers often had parents (or have) that took care of their every need and enjoyed the feeling that their kids couldn't get along without them. Worriers don't have a great deal of fun and often burn out.

SOLUTION

Deep inside most worriers lurks a more vibrant, courageous soul. If you are bored and sick of your life, that's great. You may be ready to change. When you find yourself concentrating on the risk implications in a new situation, stop and focus on what's exciting about it. Interpreting the feeling makes the difference. Next time you have butterflies in your stomach, be glad.

DEFIERS

This group of procrastinators resent authority but expresses the rebellion covertly. Ask him to do something he'll say "yes" to and then forget. Sometimes this delivers work that is half-assed or late or both in some cases. In relationships they meet their partner's needs the same way. Procrastinators often delegate their work, thus, giving them a sense of power. Their coworkers and lovers feel manipulated, used, and betrayed. When fired or stuck in dead-end jobs or relationships, the defiler consoles himself that his lot is the inevitable fate of a true individual in a fake world.

SOLUTION

Learn to act instead of react, to move from victim to active participant in life. Shift concern away from what other people are doing to you and see what you are doing to yourself.

Realize that taking the initiative – not digging in your heels is where the real power is

CRISIS-MAKERS

We do our best work under some type of time constraint. A crises-maker goes out of their way to create drama, going from one behavioral extreme to the other. He under reacts to a situation then overreacts with a big shot of intense work to meet a deadline. You can drive yourself to the edge in your 20's and 30's, but as you get older your body doesn't want to run on adrenaline anymore

SOLUTION

You need to increase self-motivation to accomplish things and decrease the emotional investment in the death-defying, last-minute performances. Recognize your need for adrenaline rush, but find a safer avenue for it than your work or your relationships. Set your sights on a five mile run or a 200 pound bench press.

PERFECTIONISTS

Basically, perfectionists are nut cases, whose self-esteem is on the line every time they do anything. Often they are idealists who are unrealistic in their use of time and energy. Deep down, the perfectionist fears nothing so much as not measuring up. If you don't play you can't lose. Procrastination is a way of putting off judgment.

SOLUTION

Experience being imperfect - and seeing the world won't end. Just once in a while goof up, it won't kill you.

OVERDOERS

Doesn't seem like a procrastinator because they are always busy. In the struggle to do it all and feel self-reliant they have no balance of work and play, drudgery and fun, personal and professional. They disappoint the people they are looking to please because of taking on so much.

SOLUTION

Need to learn to say "no". Give up the "superman myth". Accomplish what you can and leave the rest to all those "super heroes" whose work you've been doing

HOW TO EVALUATE YOUR TIME

Which activities that are on your daily time log are in line with your values and goals (refer to your goals listed in session one).

Now identify what activities on your daily time log are not in line with your values and goals.

Are any of your values being violated by any of the activities on your daily logs?

Are some of your values or goals being neglected or ignored?

Are you able to arrange your daily activities in a way that will help you in attaining your goals without jeopardizing your values?

10 TIPS TO BETTER ORGANIZATION

Use a daily calendar (provided).

Keep copies of your goals and values in a place where you will see them daily.

Keep a copy of your action plans handy to look at when needed. Included with these plans should be the rewards to yourself and others when you have completed a task.

Keep a list on you of your daily goals, including the values associated with them.

Minimize time wasters (see hints at end of session)

Get in the **habit** of saying **no**.

Make sure to allow yourself quiet time daily. You will find that you need this time to regroup.

When performing a high priority task, focus your full attention on it.

Arrange your environment, working as personal to support your goals and values.

Always reward yourself for inspiring and following your time management.

SESSION IV

IF YOU ARE NOT ENJOYING THE WORK IT IS TAKING TO ATTAIN YOUR GOALS, YOU SHOULD EITHER CHANGE YOUR ATTITUDE OR YOUR GOALS!

The fourth section is devoted to inventorying your skills. Whether thy be knowledge skills, performance skills, communication skills etc. In addition, we will discuss and write about your personal attribute and your needs for you to be successful.

Session four is time for reflection and association. First you will see if the values you have chosen in the previous session identify with any of your goals from session one. If you feel that after this review your goals are not in alignment with your values you should do some serious personal reflection about your goals. At the end of this session are some helpful ideas to get you going in identifying your goals.

If you feel that the goals you chose in session one and your values align it is time to really get down working and planning your action plan. You will be using the daily planner, the time log, and the life management calendar. Using all of these tools will help you in getting your plan started. **Remember if you fail to plan, you plan to fail.**

A few review questions to ask yourself before you begin:

Can I devote a great deal of time and energy in completing my goals as I have chosen them?

Do all of my goals fit in with the values that I have chosen?

Is this goal realistic as it relates to my life and its course I want it to take? (Use the life management calendar to see if it will work).

My goals year #1: my values as they relate

_____

_____

_____

_____

The positives and negatives of my goals in year one:
            Positives: **negatives:**

_____

_____

_____

_____

_____

Looking at this list, are these goals for year one realistic?

Check one…….. _____yes _____no

Answer the following questions:

    A. **How I decided on these goals for year 1?**

_____

_____

_____

_____

_____

_____

_____

_____

_____

_____

A. What makes them realistic to me?

_____

_____

_____

_____

_____
_____
_____

B. Are there any obstacles you can see at this time?

_____
_____
_____
_____

If so how will you overcome them?

_____
_____
_____
_____
_____
_____

C. How much time and energy do I project will it take to accomplish meeting these goals for year one?

_____
_____
_____
_____
_____
_____

Can I jeopardize these goals in any way?

_____
_____
_____
_____

What resources do I need to begin working on these goals?

_____
_____
_____

_____

_____

_____

_____

_____

Who will I ask to help me in attaining my goals for year one?

_____

_____

_____

_____

_____

_____

How will I communicate to the people the help I will need? Who what when where and why?

_____

_____

_____

_____

_____

_____

_____

_____

How will these people benefit from my goals?

_____

_____

_____

_____

_____

Can any of these people jeopardize me attaining these goals? If yes how, and how will I prevent that from happening?

_____

_____

_____

_____

_____

_____

How do I go about contacting the resources needed to attain my goals for year one?

_____

_____

_____

_____

_____

_____

_____

_____

_____

_____

_____

_____

_____

How do I communicate effectively my needs in attaining my goals for year one?

_____

_____

_____

_____

_____

_____

Are my goals and values in balance?

_____

_____

_____

Now to see if your list of goals for year one is realistic we will set up a life management calendar. The purpose is to look at your goals in a time managed system to see if you will be able to accomplish what you have set our to do. In doing this you will be able to redefine your goals that seem to be out of line with your expectations. Possibly your first year goals could be better attained if they were your goals for year two or five. This practical calendar will make that possible. It will also help in defining actions to be taken by you or others who are helping you attain your goals. Once we do this for year, one we will add the other years as we finish each exercise.

PERSONAL REFLECTION EXERCISE

Imagine you already have reached one of your goals. Now ask these questions:

How would you look, feel, behave, and sound?

_____

_____

_____

_____

_____

_____

_____

_____

_____

_____

How would others around you respond to you?

_____
_____
_____
_____
_____
_____
_____
_____
_____
_____

What steps did you take to achieve your goal?

_____
_____
_____
_____
_____
_____

Did you need to develop new skills?

_____
_____
_____
_____
_____
_____
_____
_____

How much time did it take?

_____
_____

_____

_____

_____

_____

_____

_____

What resources helped you in achieving this goal?

_____

_____

_____

_____

_____

_____

_____

How did you motivate yourself and keep going? _

_____

_____

_____

_____

_____

_____

How did you deal with obstacles you encountered?

_____

_____

_____

_____

_____

_____

Now close your eyes, review all the steps it took to achieve this goal and write them down.

_____

_____

_____

_____

_____

_____

_____

_____

_____

_____

_____

_____

_____

_____

_____

_____

_____

_____

_____

_____

_____

_____

_____

_____

_____

SESSION V

THE TWO HARDEST THINGS IN LIFE TO
HANDLE ARE FAILURE AND SUCCESS

In session five you are going to continue to identify goals and values. You will be concentrating on years 1 through 5. Depending on your goals in session four these could be your medium term goals or still your short term goals. Whichever, it is imperative to remember to follow through as you did in the last session.

Make sure your goals in this session are in balance with the goals from your previous session. Also, you will want to keep in mind that these goals are also to be in balance with your goals in future sessions.

Believe the quote, the two hardest things in life to handle are failure and success. Over time you will see this to be true if you already haven't.

Again, you will be using the life management calendar to help you in setting up your action plan. This time though the life management calendar is broken down by months not days as in session four. You will see the significance of this as you work through the workbook in setting your goals.

My goals years 1 through 5   my values as they relate

_____

_____

_____

_____

_____

_____

_____

_____

_____

_____

_____
_____
_____
_____
_____
_____
_____
_____
_____
_____
_____
_____

The positives and negatives of my goals in years 1 through 5:
Positives: negatives:

_____
_____
_____
_____
_____
_____
_____
_____
_____
_____
_____
_____
_____
_____
_____
_____
_____
_____

Looking at this, are these goals for year 1 through 5 realistic?

Check one........._____yes _____no

Answer the following questions:

A. How I decided on these goals for years 1 – 5?

_____

_____

_____

_____

_____

_____

_____

_____

_____

B. What makes them realistic to me?

_____

_____

_____

_____

_____

_____

C. Are there any obstacles you can see at this time? If so how will you overcome them?

_____

_____

_____

_____

_____

_____

D. How much time and energy do I project will it take to accomplish meeting these goals for year 1 – 5

_____

_____

_____

_____

_____

Can I jeopardize these goals in any way?

_____

_____

_____

_____

_____

_____

_____

_____

_____

_____

What resources do I need to begin working on these goals?

_____

_____

_____

_____

_____

_____

_____

_____

_____

Who will I ask to help me in attaining my goals for year 1 –5?

_____

_____

_____

_____

_____

_____

_____

_____

_____

_____

How will I communicate to these people the help I will need?

_____

_____

_____

_____

_____

How will these people benefit from my goals?

_____

_____

_____

_____

_____

_____

Can any of these people jeopardize me attaining these goals? If yes how, and how will I prevent that happening?

_____

_____

_____

_____

_____

_____

How do I go about contacting the resources needed to attain my goals for
year 1 – 5?

_____

_____

_____

_____

_____

_____

_____

_____

_____

_____

_____

How do I communicate effectively my needs in attaining my goals for
year 1 – 5?

_____

_____

_____

_____

_____

Are my goals and values in balance?

_____

_____

_____

_____

_____

_____

_____

_____

Now to see if your list of goals for year one through five is realistic we will set up a life management calendar. The purpose is to look at your goals in a time managed system to see if you will be able to accomplish what you have set out to do. In doing this you will be able to redefine your goals that seem to be out of line with your expectations. Possibly your goals in years one through five could be better achieved in years five through ten or even in your first years. This practical calendar will make that possible. It will also help in defining actions to be taken by you or others who are helping you attain your goals.

SESSION VI

WHEN YOU COME TO A FORK IN THE ROAD TAKE IT!

YOGI BERRA

STATED TO THE GRADUATES OF MONTCLAIR STATE UNIVERSITY IN 1996

Session 6....... The rest of this program is up to you. We will use this time to review what you have accomplished and answer any questions you have regarding your plan.

Don't be afraid to ask questions. It is the only way to get ahead. You have come a long way in the last six weeks. If you have come this far, you want to succeed. So don't stop. Don't take short cuts. Don't make excuses. Don't procrastinate. Don't give up.......

Remember; do give up your bad habits. Do pick up new habits. Do organize your day. Do follow through with your plan. Do take the fork in the road.

DO SUCCEED!!

MY GOALS YEARS 5 THROUGH 10   MY VALUE AS THEY RELATE

_____

_____

_____

_____

_____

_____

_____

_____

THE POSITIVES AND NEGATIVES OF MY GOALS IN YEARS 5
THROUGH 10:

POSITIVES: NEGATIVES:

_____

_____

_____

_____

LOOKING AT THIS LIST, ARE THESE GOALS FOR YEARS 5
THROUGH 10 REALISTIC?

Check one………. _____yes _____ no

Answer the following questions:

How I decided on these goals for years 5 – 10?

_____

_____

_____

_____

_____

_____

_____

_____

_____

What makes them realistic to me?

_____

_____

_____

_____

_____

_____

Are there any obstacles you can see at this time? If so how will you overcome them?

_____

How much time and energy do I project will it take to accomplish meeting these goals for years 5 – 10?

_____
_____

Can I jeopardize these goals in any way?

_____
_____
_____
_____
_____
_____

What resources do I need to begin working on these goals?

_____
_____
_____
_____
_____
_____
_____

Who will I ask to help me in attaining my goals for year 5 – 10?

_____
_____
_____
_____
_____
_____
_____

How will I communicate to these people the help I will need?

_____
_____
_____
_____
_____
_____
_____
_____

How will these people benefit from my goal?

_____
_____
_____
_____
_____
_____
_____
_____
_____
_____
_____
_____

Can any of these people jeopardize me attaining these goals? If yes how, and how will I prevent that happening?

_____
_____
_____
_____
_____
_____
_____

Ann Anderson

How do I go about contacting the resources needed to attain my goals for years 5 – 10?

_____
_____
_____
_____
_____
_____
_____
_____
_____
_____

How do I communicate effectively my needs in attaining my goals for years 5 -10?

_____
_____
_____
_____
_____
_____
_____

Are my goals and values in balance?

_____
_____
_____
_____
_____
_____
_____
_____
_____
_____

Now to see if your list of goals for year five through ten is realistic we will set up a life management calendar. The purpose is to look at your goals in a time managed system to see if you will be able to accomplish what you have set out to do. In doing this you will be able to redefine your goals that seem to be out of line with your expectations. Possibly your goals in years five through ten could be better achieved in years ten through twenty or even in years one through five. This practical calendar will make that possible. It will also help in defining actions to be taken by you or others who are helping you attain your goals.

My goals years 10 through 20   my values as they relate

_____

_____

_____

_____

_____

_____

_____

_____

_____

_____

_____

_____

_____

_____

_____

The positives and negatives of my goals in years 10 through 20:

Positives: negatives:

_____

_____

_____

_____

Looking at this list, are these goals for years 10 through 20 realistic?

Check one........ _____yes _____no

Answer the following questions:

A. How I decided on these goals for years 10 – 20?

_____

_____

_____

_____

B. What makes them realistic to me?

_____

_____

_____

C. Are there any obstacles you can see at this time? If so how will you overcome them?

_____

_____

D. How much time and energy do I project will it take to accomplish meeting these goals for years 10 –20?

_____

_____

_____

Can I jeopardize these goals in any way?

_____

_____

_____

_____

_____

_____

_____

_____

_____

_____

What resources do I need to begin working on these goals?

_____

_____

_____

_____

_____

_____

Who will I ask to help me in attaining my goals for years 10 – 20?

_____

_____

_____

_____

_____

_____

_____

_____

_____

How will I communicate to these people the help I will need?

_____

_____

_____

_____

_____

_____

_____

_____

_____

How will these people benefit from my goals?

_____

_____

_____

_____

_____

_____

Can any of these people jeopardize me attaining these goals? If yes how, and how will I prevent that happening?

_____

_____

_____

_____

How do I go about contacting the resources needed to attain my goals for years 10 – 20?

_____

_____

_____

How do I communicate effectively my needs in attaining my goals for years 10 –20?

_____

_____

_____

_____

_____

_____

_____

_____

_____

_____

Are my goals and values in balance?

_____

_____

Now to see if your list of goals for year ten through twenty is realistic we will set up a life management calendar. The purpose is to look at your goals in a time managed system to see if you will be able to accomplish what you have set out to do. In doing this you will be able to redefine your goals that seem to be out of line with your expectations. Possibly your goals in years ten through twenty would be better achieved over a longer time period or even be achieved during your earlier years. This practical calendar will make that possible. It will also help in defining actions to be taken by you or others who are helping you attain your goals.

APPENDIX A

DAILYTIME LOG

ACTIVITY	TIME
DAILY TIME LOG	

USE THIS DAILY FOR ONE WEEK. AT THE END OF THE WEEK REVIEW, THE ACTIVITIES AND THE AMOUNT OF TIME YOU SPENT ON THEM. ASK YOURSELF IF THESE ACTIVITES ARE IN ALIGNMENT WITH YOUR GOALS AND VALUES. IF NOT MAKE THE NECESSARY CHANGES SO THAT YOU CAN ACCOMPLISH YOUR GOALS.

APPENDIX B

DAILY PLANNER

DAILY PLANNER   DATE: _____

6:00 _____

7:00 _____

8:00 _____

9:00 _____

10:00 _____

11:00 _____

12:00 _____

1:00 _____

2:00 _____

3:00 _____

4:00 _____

5:00 _____

6:00 _____

7:00 _____

8:00 _____

9:00 _____

10:00 _____

TO DO TODAY:

_____   _____

_____   _____

APPENDIX C

WEEKLY PLANNER   **WEEK OF** _____

TO DO AND REMARKS
MONDAY
TUESDAY
WEDNESDAY
THURSDAY
FRIDAY
SATURDAY
SUNDAY

MONTHLY MANGEMENT LIFE CALENDAR

LIFE MANAGEMENT CALENDAR
MONTH_____ GOAL_____

ACTIVITY/ASSIGNED				

APPENDIX E

YEARLY GOALS CALANDAR

**LIFE MANAGEMENT CALENDAR YEAR_____ GOAL
ACTIVITY/ASSIGNED**

APPENDIX F

SUCCESS CHART

SUCCESS	
ALTERNATE PATH	
ALTERNATE PATH	
ALTERNATE PATH	
ALTERNATE PATH	
ALTERNATE PATH	
ALTERNATE PATH	
ALTERNATE PATH	
ALTERNATE PATH	
ALTERNATE PATH	
ALTERNATE PATH	

STRESS

**We may indeed be creatures of habit but no matter how hard we
work to control our environment, the unexpected will always
overtake us. We have to accept that we can't control every
aspect of our lives, and make adjustments when need be. It is
the little stressors that were us down: the almost, the might-
have-been, the could-should-would. Flexibility is the key.**

PROBLEMS WITH YOUR LIFE BEING IN UTTER CHAOS?

FOLLOWING THESE LITTLE TIPS TO HELP!

DAY ONE: drink peppermint or lemon tea. If you can't do that, use visualization techniques and pretend. Research has shown that the smelling of the scents of lemon or peppermint can make you feel slightly relaxed.

Day two: practice the "one-breath" meditation technique. When that stress arrives just sit up straight in a comfortable position, relax your shoulders, take a breath, and inhale deeply to open your chest. While doing this imagine that the breath is filling every cell in your body.

Day three: try on this day if the stress is still there, the one touch relaxation technique. Place your second finger against your thumb until the stress leaves. As you continue to do this and feel relaxed, remember these feelings, and whenever the stress shows up press these two fingers together. If all else fails, go outside, and give a good scream.

Day four: another breathing trick is to inhale; clench your teeth for five seconds, AND then exhale. Let your jaw muscles go loose and say "aahhhh". Your jaw muscle is the most powerful muscle in your body. If you can learn to tense and then relax, it should cause a cascading relaxation effect throughout your body.

Day five:	take today to go outside and stand in the sun. Of course if there is no sun, go back to day three and give a good scream outside. If the sun is out though, standing a good 10 to 15 minutes in the sunshine will have a dramatic effect on your mood and stress level.
Day six:	now we get to the good part. Today, crank out a good abdominal exercise. It is not only relaxing but it will help to tone your stomach. Of course, it will also help in getting that extra stress of the day out of your system. If this is not your idea of a stress reliever, try your own for the day.
Day seven:	try liming--this term comes from the Caribbean meaning, to do nothing. Do nothing rest free for the day. It should give your brain a chance to unwind as well as your body. Remember, your brain also can get overloaded as well as your body. Give stresses a battle. Don't let it get to you.

Never say...

1. **"They didn't get back to me" or "they are getting back to me". Expecting someone to get back to you stops the action. Take the initiative.**
2. **"I thought someone else was taking care of that." Excuses indicate a roadblock to action. Always ask questions to keep things moving.**
3. **"No one ever told me". By saying this to yourself over and over, you try to justify actions that will keep you operating in a tunnel. Don't operate in a tunnel.**
4. **"I didn't have time". "I was too busy." If you find yourself saying these things you're writing your own obituary for excuses in life.**
5. **"I didn't think to ask about that." The inability to see down the road may indicate that you lack the ability to understand and grasps relationships.**

Reacting to difficult types...

Dealing with the aggressor, who is intimidating, hostile and loves to threaten...

Listen to everything the person has to say. Avoid arguments and be formal, calling the person by name. Be concise and clear with your reactions.

Dealing with the undermines who takes pride in criticisms and is sarcastic and devour...
Focus on the issues and don't acknowledge sarcasm. Don't overreact.

Dealing with the unresponsive person, who is difficult to talk to and never reveals their ideas... ask open-ended questions and learn to be silent-waiting for the person to say something. Be patient and friendly.

Dealing with the egotist, who knows it all, and feels and acts superior... Make sure you know the facts. Agree when possible and ask questions and listen. Disagree only when you know you are right.

ACKNOWLEDGEMENTS

All quotes used on title pages are adapted from **Leadership Magazine,** a publication of the economic press Inc.

The list of personalities used in session three were adapted for this program from the March 1997 issue of M**en's Health Magazine.**

The life management calendar was adapted from software developed by **Opera Software Publishing, Inc.**

Some of the concepts in this workbook were adapted from **The Relaxation and Stress Reduction Workbook,** 4th Edition, A New Harbinger Publication, Inc.

Dynamic Paradigm Management is for Family members, business men and women and homemakers who are looking to just redefine their life. People like you and me who want to accomplish their goals. So don't sit there and think it will not work because you are incarcerated. This is actually the best time to put all your thoughts and goals down in written form to work them out and come to a conclusion. What the heck, you have the time to put it to positive use.

Remember to keep your ideas, goals, and values, positive. No negative goals are ever accomplished with a successful ending. Look at where we are now.

Again as I said before, I have used this program. I did not just sit down and write it from my head. It has been in use for the past several years. I follow it and practice it as a philosophy. Finally, that "yes", I was able to accomplish my goals no matter how surreal they were.

If during this course you have questions in regards to my use of the program. Ask. Never let a question go unanswered. It could be important to your success. That is what we are here for –our success.

Let us succeed together. I will answer your questions to the best of my ability, regarding my feelings and thoughts on how I answered these same questions.

		Time Management- Week of __/__/__							
	Sun	Mon	Tue	Wed	Thur	Fri	Sat	
Time									
7:00 - 8:00AM									
8:00 - 9:00AM									
9:00 - 10:00AM									
10:00 - 11:00AM									
11:00 - 12:00PM									
12:00 - 1:00PM									
1:00 - 2:00PM									
2:00 - 3:00PM									
3:00 - 4:00PM									
4:00 - 5:00PM									
5:00 - 6:00PM									
6:00 - 7:00PM									
7:00 - 8:00PM									

8:00 - 9:00PM								
Goal Daily Dials								
# Dials								
# Contacts								
# Messages Left								
# Not Interested								
# Demos Booked								
# 30 min								
# 3ways								
#LOIs								
NOTES AND MEMO'S								

Major Definite Purpose Major Definite Purpose – Self Confidence Formula This is a formula from the book Think and Grow Rich by Napoleon Hill

My Major Definite Purpose

By the first day of (_____) 201____, I **will** have in my possession $_____ monthly residual income which will come to me in various amounts from time to time during the interim.

In exchange for this money I will give the most efficient service of which I am capable, rendering the fullest possible quantity and best possible quality of service in the capacity of (_____).

I believe that I will have this money in my possession. My faith is **so strong** that I can now see this money before my eyes. I can touch it with my hands. It is now awaiting transfer to me at the time and in the proportion that I deliver the service I intend to render for it. I am awaiting a plan by which to accumulate this money, and I will follow that plan, when it is received. Major Definite Purpose – Self Confidence Formula

FAMOUS QUOTES

Sometimes, when I look at my children, I say to myself, "Lillian,
You should have remained a virgin."
- Lillian Carter (mother of 64ᵗʰ Jimmy Carter)

I had a rose named after me and I was very flattered. But I was not
Pleased to read the description in the catalog: "No good in a bed, but
Fine against a wall."
- Eleanor Roosevelt

The secret of a good sermon is to have a good beginning and a good
ending; and to have the two as close together as possible.
- George Burns

Santa Claus has the right idea. Visit people only once a year.
- Victor Borge

Be careful about reading health books. You may die of a misprint.
- Mark Twain

By all means, marry. If you get a good wife, you'll become happy; if you
get a bad one, you'll become a philosopher.
- Socrates

I was married by a judge. I should have asked for a jury.
- Groucho Marx

The male is a domestic animal which, if treated with firmness and kindness,
can be trained to do most things.
- Jilly Cooper

I have never hated a man enough to give his diamonds back.
- Zsa Zsa Gabor

Only Irish coffee provides in a single glass all four essential food groups: alcohol, caffeine, sugar and fat.

    - Alex Levine

Don't go around saying the world owes you a living. The world owes you nothing. It was here first.

    - Mark Twain

My luck is so bad that if I bought a cemetery, people would stop dying.

    - Ed Furgol

Money can't buy you happiness... but it does bring you a more pleasant form of misery.

    - Spike Milligan

What's the use of happiness? It can't buy you money.

    - Henny Youngman

Until I was thirteen, I thought my name was shut up.

    - Joe Namath

Youth would be an ideal state if it came a little later in life.

    - Herbert Henry Asquith

I don't feel old. I don't feel anything until noon. Then it's time for my nap.

    - Bob Hope

I never drink water because of the disgusting things that fish do in it.

    - WC. Fields

We could certainly slow the aging process down if it had to work its way through Congress.

    - Will Rogers

Don't worry about avoiding temptation... as you grow older, it will avoid you.

    - Winston Churchill

Maybe it's true that life begins at fifty... but everything else starts to wear out, fall out, or spread out.
- Phyllis Diller

The cardiologist's diet: If it tastes good spit it out.
- Unknown

By the time a man is wise enough to watch his step, he's too old to go anywhere. - Billy Crystal

Robert Kyosaki and Donald Trump Want You Rich

"You can make excuses or you can make money...you can't make both!"

— Donald Trump

— "Network marketing has proven itself to be a viable and rewarding source of income, and the challenges could be just right for you. There have been some remarkable examples of success, and those successes have been earned through diligence, enthusiasm and the right product combined with timing."

— Donald Trump

Economic Advisor To Two U.S. Presidents Calls It "A 21st Century 'Millionaire Population' Explosion..."

"In the 10 years from 1991 to 2001, the number of U.S. millionaire households doubled, from 3.6 million to 7.2 million. In the ten years from 2006 to 2016, we're on track to more than double that number by creating another 10 million millionaires, for a total of more than 18.5 million millionaires!

We're witnessing nothing less than a millionaire population explosion in the 21st Century and it is all due to THIS business model. This community is a group that often picks up on trends long before the rest of the world has noticed them."

— Paul Zane Pilzer

Economist, Best Selling Author
Economic Advisor to two U.S. presidents

Here are five things that research has shown can improve happiness:
1. **<u>Be grateful</u>**
2. **<u>Be optimistic</u>**
3. **<u>Count your blessings</u>**
4. **<u>Use your strengths</u>**
5. **<u>Commit acts of kindness</u>**

Andy Rooney

May comfort, joy and peace be with you through the years to come. Take this knowledge of wisdom with you as you have made a special part in my life. Peace and joy be with you always,

WITH LOVE AND BLESSINGS FROM THE HEART, Forever and always your friend.

ANN ANDERSON

GOLDEN STAIRS AND STEPPING STONES

I am but a timid soul
In need of your hand to hold.
As time goes by
I feel the need to cry.

Every little heartache felt,
Each disappointment roughly dealt.
Always trusting to the end.
On God's strength I can depend.

May every silent pain I bear,
Become to me a golden stair.
That raises high above the glow,
For you to love and you to know.

That through it all you will see,
A fire that burns for me.
Afloat the boat in which I ride,
Until I reach the other side.

From life's waters dark and deep,
Your blessed presents I will keep.
Upon your strength I can depend,
Amid the trials you have sent.

I know my tears and sighs and groans,
Are only God's little stepping stones.
God please let me understand and see
Everything that is meant for me.

I know that every prayer is one more step,
Of patients, love and understanding of your prep.
Until the day I am laid to rest,
Performing daily, I will do my best.
ANN ANDERSON

You can't read this and stay in a bad mood!
1. How Do You Catch a Unique Rabbit? Unique Up On It.
2. How Do You Catch a Tame Rabbit? Tame Way, Unique Up On It.
3. How Do Crazy People Go Through The Forest? They Take The Psycho Path
4. How Do You Get Holy Water? You Boil The Hell Out Of It.
5. What Do Fish Say When They Hit a Concrete Wall? Dam!
6. What Do Eskimos Get From Sitting On The Ice too Long? Polaroid's
7. What Do You Call a Boomerang That Doesn't work? A Stick
8. What Do You Call Cheese That Isn't Yours? Nacho Cheese.
9. What Do You Call Santa's Helpers? Subordinate Clauses.
10. What Do You Call Four Bullfighters In Quicksand? Quattro Sinko.
11. What Do You Get From a Pampered Cow? Spoiled Milk.
12. What Do You Get When You Cross a Snowman With a Vampire? Frostbite.
13. What Lies At The Bottom Of The Ocean And Twitches? A Nervous Wreck.
14. What's The Difference Between Roast Beef And Pea Soup? Anyone Can Roast Beef.
15. Where Do You Find a Dog With No Legs? Right Where You Left Him.
16. Why Do Gorillas Have Big Nostrils? Because They Have Big Fingers.

17. Why Don't Blind People Like To Sky Dive? Because It Scares The Dog.

18. What Kind Of Coffee Was Served On The Titanic? Sanka.

19. What Is The Difference Between a Harley And a Hoover?
The Location Of The Dirt Bag.

20. Why Did Pilgrims' Pants Always Fall Down?
Because They Wore Their Belt Buckle On Their Hat.

21. What's The Difference Between a Bad Golfer And a Bad Skydiver?
A Bad Golfer Goes, "Whack, Dang!"
A Bad Skydiver Goes, "Dang! Whack."

22. How Are a Texas Tornado And a Tennessee Divorce The Same?
Somebody's Gonna Lose A Trailer

Now, admit it. At least one of these made you smile, maybe two!

Subject: Beer Warning.....Plus Video

Two Friends

Today's your special day-
the start of both your lives, together.
May it be special in every way
sparked by the love you've treasured
and may all the love you're feeling
still find a way to grow,
sharing joys which have a meaning
that only both of you could know.

May God bless your health
as you care for each other's needs,
may you both share in the wealth
of raising a family,
may your new dreams never end-
we hope they all come true,

and may you always be two friends
who have your love, each day, be new.

Again, today is your day,
with the bond between you strong.
God has shown both of you the way
and placed his love where it belongs
and as you hold on to each other
always keeping your love dear,
know you're blessed both by the Father
and each one of us who's here.

Today two friends start a journey
walking hand in hand, as one
they'll share everything, always
now that their journey has begun
and as they go on together,
blessed by me and you,
may these two friends always treasure
the day they said, "I do."

Take care & God Bless....Do you listen: when you hear these things: (I do)....

Universal Mother's
Mother's must celebrate everyday.
To all the women of the world. We celebrate life.
May God be with you and your children throughout their life and beyond,
for peace, health and happiness to bless each and everyone you come in
contact with
For the safety and well beings of your families.
Give them strength and courage to withstand all pressures and pains of life
As a learning curve to make them be a better person for themselves and
their loved ones. Keep them spiritually happy,
While giving them the wisdom and the knowledge to withstand and
conquer the enemies to a victorious victory.

All women are mothers even if they do not have children.
We are all angels in the flesh helping one another and teaching others to do their best. Women stand out as the powerful love bonds us all together. Mothers have to pass on this wisdom of truth forever.
For without us no one would survive.
I say this with Love and Prayers
To all the mothers and mothers who want to be mothers,
And all the women who love in the world that love come from Mothers.
Happy Mother's Day! Ann Anderson, May 8, 2008

I truly hope that all your plans and dreams Become your faith in front of the screen You will always be in my heart and spirit wishing you happiness of your success.

With love and Peace and in my prayers, your friend forever, I remain
ANN ANDERSON

PROSPERITY

'DON'T BELIEVE A WORD I SAY.'
Why would I suggest that? Because I can only come from my own experience. Meaning that nothing I say is inherently true or false, right or wrong. It's just my experience.

The principles I teach in my seminars have totally transformed my life, and have now transformed the lives for over four years now. And if you learn these principles, and more importantly use them, they can **transform your life too**.

SO WHAT IS MY EXPERIENCE?
I began designing programs based on the 'inner' game of money and success and when we combined the inner game (the toolbox) with the outer game (the tools), virtually everybody's results went through the roof! And that's what you're going to 'learn': **how to blend the inner game with the outer game to achieve total success.**

Josh Billings put it this way; 'It's not what we don't know that prevents us from succeeding, it's what we know that <u>just ain't so</u> that is our greatest obstacle.'

LEARNING TO UNLEARN
Therefore, it's not only about 'learning,' it's also about 'unlearning!' It's important to realize that your old ways of thinking and being have gotten you exactly where you are right now. If you're really rich and really happy, fine. But if you're not, I'd invite you to consider some possibilities that may not fit into what you 'think' is right.

One of my favorite stories is a perfect example of how most people search for answers in life, but when the answers don't fit with their old ways of thinking they simply ignore them and continue searching.

A man who is walking along a cliff all of a sudden loses his balance, slips and falls off, but he has the presence of mind to grab on to the ledge. He's hanging there for dear life. He's hanging and hanging and finally calls out, 'Is there anybody up there that can help me? There's no answer. He keeps calling and calling and finally this big bellowing voice calls back, 'This is God. I can help you. Just let go and trust.' Next thing you hear, 'Is there anybody else up there that can help me?'

Whether it's by 'learning' or 'unlearning', if you're ready to develop a 'millionaire mind' and **move quickly towards true wealth and happiness in your life**, then read on.

- **Why many people tend to 'blow up' their successes.**
- **The meaning and power of the acronym 'TFAR'.**
- **Why not having enough money is never, ever a problem.**

I explained earlier that people exposed to the same "outer world" wealth creation tools produce different results. When I began to add processes to help people develop their "inner world," the way they think and feel about wealth, virtually **everyone's results went through the roof.**

I want to challenge you with an idea:
YOUR OLD WAYS OF THINKING AND BEING HAVE GOTTEN YOU EXACTLY WHERE YOU ARE RIGHT NOW.

If you're really rich and really happy, fine. But if you're not, I'd invite you to consider some possibilities that may not fit into what you "think" is right.

THE MEANING AND POWER OF THE ACRONYM 'TFAR'

"The Roots Create The Fruits"

Imagine a tree. Let's suppose this tree represents the tree of life. On this tree there are fruits. In real life our fruits are called our results. So we look at the fruits (our results) and we don't like them. We think there's not enough of them or they're too small or they don't taste good.

So what do we do? Most of us put even more attention and focus on the fruits; our results. But what is it that actually creates those particular fruits? It's the seeds and the roots that create those fruits. It's what's under the ground that creates what's above the ground. It's the invisible that creates the visible. Meaning that if you want to change the fruits, you will first have to change the roots.

In order to change your roots, let me introduce you to a very important formula. This formula is so critical that understanding it can change your life! It is called the Process of Manifestation:

T-> F-> A-> R Thoughts, Feelings, Actions, Results
Thoughts lead to Feelings.
Feelings lead to Actions.
Actions lead to Results.

If you want to change your results, your "Fruits", your will need to change your thoughts, your "roots."
This will help you understand why...

NOT HAVING ENOUGH MONEY IS NEVER, EVER A PROBLEM!

Not having enough money is a RESULT! If a problem exists, it's in your thinking and how that thinking manifests through feelings and actions to produce your results.

SO WHAT DO YOU DO?

I'm known for saying "Give me five minutes and I can predict your financial future for the rest of your life."
How? In a short conversation, I can identify what's called your money and success "blueprint." Each of us has a personal money and success blueprint already ingrained in our subconscious mind and this blueprint will determine your financial destiny.

So what is a blueprint? Consider the blueprint for a house. The blueprint is a preset plan or design for that particular home.

In the same way, your "money blueprint" is simply a preset program or way of being in relation to money. And through the TFAR formula, **your blueprint manifests your financial reality**.

In the next installment of the Secret Psychology of Wealth newsletter, we'll look in more depth into the following topics:

- **How your Money Blueprint is formed.**
- **What the 3 primary methods of conditioning are.**
- **What is your Money Blueprint set for?**

We discovered that people have a subconscious capacity for financial success which often results in their "blowing" wealth or wealth building opportunities: in short, **your wealth can only "grow" to the extent that you do**.

Further, we discovered the LAW OF MANIFESTATION and the acronym, TFAR, which means that your Thoughts (core beliefs - subconscious) lead to Feelings which lead to Actions which produce your Results. And naturally from this we can see that **a lack of money is never a "problem,"** it's a result of conditioned and largely automatic thinking.

This carries us to today's topic which will **help you determine the source of your subconscious thoughts**, namely your personal money and success blueprint.

HOW YOUR MONEY BLUEPRINT IS FORMED.
As I mentioned last week, your "money blueprint' is simply a preset program or way of being in relation to money.
Your financial blueprint consists of your thoughts, feelings and actions in the arena of money. Notice that these are based in your "inner" world, and that they lead to your results, which are based in your outer world.

So how do you get your money blueprint? The answer is simple.
Your financial blueprint consists primarily of the "programming" you received in your past, especially as a young child.

Who were the primary sources of this conditioning? They were parents, siblings, friends, authority figures, teachers, religious leaders, media, and your culture to name a few. Take culture. Isn't it true that certain cultures have a certain way of thinking and dealing with money while in other cultures it's completely different?

Do you think a child comes out of the womb with those ways of being? No. The child is **"taught"** how to think about and act in relation to money. The same holds true for you. You were "taught" how to think about and handle money, whether you realized it at the time or not. Then you take this conditioning with you and run on it for the rest of your life.

HOW TO BECOME SUCCESSFUL AUTOMATICALLY.

Becoming automatically successful means changing your present programming which may not be set for success and replacing it with programming that is. If you're set to struggle for wealth because you are programmed to believe wealth only comes from struggle and hard work, you can then change your beliefs to make money "easy," to **make yourself a "money & success magnet."**
But before you can change your programming you need to become self "aware." The first element of all change is "awareness." Become "conscious." Watch yourself. Observe your thoughts, your beliefs, your fears, your habits, your actions, your inactions. Put yourself under a microscope. Study yourself.

It's funny. As intelligent human beings we think that we live our lives based on "choice." This is not usually the case. If we are truly enlightened we might make a few present moment choices during the average day, but for the most part, we're like robots, running on automatic, ruled by our past conditioning and old habits.

That's where awareness, or consciousness, comes in. Consciousness is observing yourself and your thought processes so you can live from true choice in the present moment rather than programming from the past. So you can live from who you are today rather than who you were yesterday. So you can respond wisely to situations rather than react wildly.

Once you are "conscious" you can see your programming for what it is; simply a recording of information you received and believed in the past, when you were too young to know any better. You can see that this conditioning is not who you are but who you "learned" to be.

You can see that you are not the "recording" but the "recorder." You are not the "contents" in the glass, but the "glass" itself. You can see that you started off "empty", with a clean slate, and were filled up with other people's beliefs.

Again, beliefs are not true or false or right or wrong, they are merely opinions that have been passed down from generation to generation to you. Knowing this, you can choose to release any thought, belief or way of being that is not supportive to your wealth and replace it with one that is.

You can adopt new beliefs; rich beliefs. Remember, thoughts lead to feelings which lead to actions which lead to results. **You can choose to think and act like rich people do and therefore create the results that rich people create.**

DISCOVER THE IMPORTANCE OF RICH THINKING.

Rich people have a way of thinking that is different from poor and middle class people. They think differently about money, wealth, themselves, other people, and life. We're going to examine some of the differences between how rich people think and how poor or middle class people think.

By doing so, you will have some alternative beliefs in the files of your mind from which to choose. In this way, you can catch yourself thinking as poor people do and quickly switch over to how rich people think. Remember, beliefs are not right, wrong, true or false, they're just past opinions which can be changed on your command. The fact is, **you can CHOOSE to think in ways that will support you instead of ways that don't.**

A few caveats: first, in no way, shape or form do I mean to degrade poor people or be without compassion for their position. I do not believe rich people are "better" than the poor, they're just richer. At the same time, I want to make certain you get the most from this so I'm going to make the distinctions between the rich and poor as extreme as possible.

Second, when I refer to rich, poor and middle class "people" what I am referring to is their "mentalities"; how they think and how they act.

Third, I will be generalizing "big time." I understand not "all" rich and not "all" poor people are the way I'm describing them. Again, my objective is to make sure you understand the principles being taught here. Don't bother figuring out whether you agree or disagree with every word. Just use what pertains to you. (My guess is it's more than you might want to admit.)

Fourth, for the most part, I will not be referring to the "middle class" specifically. The reason for this is that usually middle class people have somewhat of a mix of both the rich and poor mentalities. Again, just see where you fit in on the scale and if you want to create a lot more financial success, think more like the "rich."

Fifth, several of the principles in this section appear to have more to do with habits and actions than ways of thinking. Remember the process of manifestation, which states that our actions come from our feelings which come from our thoughts. Therefore, every "rich" action is preceded by a "rich" way of thinking.

PRACTICE THINKING RICH

Sixth, each "rich" way of thinking will be reinforced by a "Declaration" at the end of the section.

Declarations are simply statements you say aloud. They are extremely valuable because everything is energy and each declaration carries its own energy and vibrational frequency.

When you state the declaration aloud, its energy vibrates through your body and into your "being". This is a way you can transform your cells of memory, your conditioning, your beliefs, and eventually your habits and actions.

State your declaration each morning and evening. Declaring into a mirror will accelerate the process.

I understand you might perceive "Declarations" to be a bit "hokey". Maybe so, but they work. Regardless, **I'd rather be "hokey and rich" than "cool and broke"**. How about you?

Finally, the concepts you are about to learn are simple but profound. They make real changes for real people in the real world. How do I know? We get thousands of letters and emails each year telling us how each and every one of these principles has transformed people's lives. If you learn them, and use them, they will transform your life too.

So here's an opportunity to Think Rich right now. Say the following Declaration out loud to yourself (into a mirror is ideal):

"TO CHANGE MY OUTER WORLD, I MUST FIRST CHANGE MY INNER WORLD."

HOW YOU DO ANYTHING IS HOW YOU DO EVERYTHING

So how did you do? Did you say the declaration out loud? Did you embrace it as a new idea worthy of your consideration? Or did you decide to continue reading and ignore the practice as being "not for me?"

Naturally, saying declarations alone is not sufficient to totally replace your current programming, but it's a valuable step. More importantly, your willingness to embrace this time tested and proven process is the key to your general willingness to embrace any changes that will **help you achieve what you truly deserve--unlimited abundance!**

In the next Secret Psychology of Wealth we will be looking at 3 specific ways in which the rich think differently than the poor. In fact, as a head start, below are the three declarations we will conclude with next week:

- **I create the exact amount of my wealth!**
- **My goal is to create extreme wealth and abundance!**
- **I commit to being rich**
  Today I will explain three more "rich" ways of thinking and will conclude each with one of the following Declarations:
- **I think big! I choose to serve a massive amount of people!**
- **I am bigger than any problem.**
- **I see the opportunities in everything.**

We introduced three primary ways that the rich think differently than the poor. And to begin the process of manifesting change in your life I offered you three "Attitudes of Wealth" affirmations to say daily.

In brief I pointed out that rich people take complete responsibility for their lives. They understand that they're not victims but are in fact the architects of their own failure and success.

Secondly, we revealed that rich people **"play" the money "game" to win** while the poor generally play the money game "not to lose." The poor generally are focused on just paying the bills, having a few "comforts" and getting by month to month. So that's what the universe continues to send them, just enough to get by.

Finally, we clarified that rich people are committed to being rich and that is why they manifest wealth. Unless you are committed both consciously and unconsciously to achieving wealth, you will experience real world results which reflect your degree of commitment.

So, are you ready to round this series off with three more insights into the Millionaire Mind? Lets go!

RICH PEOPLE THINK BIG.
Poor people think small.

We once had a trainer teaching at one of our seminars who went from a net worth of $250 thousand to over $600 million in only 3 years. When asked his secret he said, "Everything changed the day I began to think big."

In my book, Speed Wealth, I discuss the "Law of Income" which states that "you will be paid in direct proportion to the value you deliver according to the market place."

Another way of understanding this is to answer the following question: How many people do you actually serve or affect?

For instance in my business, some trainers enjoy speaking to groups of 20, others are comfortable with 100, others like an audience of 500, still others want 5000 people or more in attendance. Is there is a difference in income between these trainers? You bet there is.

Who are you? How do you want to live your life? How do you want to play the game? Do you want to play in the big leagues or in little league, in the majors or the minors? Will you play big or play small? It's your choice.

The truth is most people choose to play small. Why?

First, fear. They're scared to death of either failure or success.

Second is unworthiness. They feel small. They don't feel they're good enough or important enough to make a big difference.

But hear this. It's not about you. It's about living your mission. It's about living true to your purpose. It's about adding your piece of the puzzle to the world. It's about serving others. Most of us are so stuck in our egos that everything revolves around "me, me and more me." But again, it's not about you, **it's about adding value to other people's lives**.

Buckminster Fuller said, "The purpose of our lives is to add value to the people of this generation and those that follow."

The goal is to **share your gifts and value with as many people as possible**.

To paraphrase Nelson Mandela, "The world doesn't need more people, playing small."

It's your choice. One road leads to being broke and miserable, the other leads to money, meaning, and fulfillment.

It's time to stop hiding out and start stepping out. It's time to stop needing and start leading. It's time to start being the star that you are. It's time to share your gifts and value in a BIG way.

There could be thousands or even millions of people counting on you. Are you up to the challenge for our society and our children's sake? Let's hope so.

Please feel free to google how to live a happier life by choosing to be Happy at all times.

If you want to be happy you must choose to be happy! Learn the secrets of the Laws of Attraction to live by. Being grateful by waking up and saying "Thank You" for all you have and all you are and who you are and who you are yet to be… Thanking your creators. Let it be with God and to his glory to be in his glory for which you are to become. Send out thank you letters means a lot to anyone who has helped you on your way to succeed. Whatever your goals are, let it be to his power for the Knowledge, wisdom, strength, courage and peace that you have obtained by wanting it. Ask and you shall receive…be it to his glory. Get into a good Bible base church and count your blessings every day.

Visualize yourself with a vision board with the family home and cars you wish to acquire. Or visualize the office you wish to be working in and the school you wish to attend. Maybe it is a vacation you wish for and how you will acquire the funds to take that dream vacation. Use your talents to visualize what you want in life. Dreams are just dreams until you write them down and plan. Goals begins with a plan short term and long term goals that create habits to obtain whatever strength, knowledge courage and wisdom with peace and joy including the struggles it takes to get where you want to be.

Be kind and optimistic! Treat people the way you would like to be treated yourself. By dreaming it and knowing in your heart that you can achieve it whatever you dream can be yours if you plan. Make small steps to achieve your goals. Be patient and loving and kind to yourself. Write down your long term goals and work backwards. How long will it take you to achieve that goal? Be honest if you have to obtain a degree and what classes it takes to achieve a degree or certification. How many years will it take and what will you do to supplement your income for living from day to day. Figure out a budget and who will be there to support you and work with you, or will you do it solo. A budget that is sustainable with today's economy may require some financial skill or a person that can help you figure those costs out. Google is a great tool and resources are available online for some idea of cost of living and income requirements. It does help to have a supportive loving partner who accepts you and loves you unconditionally no matter what is in your past or in theirs. You must learn to reciprocate that unconditional transfer of love and acceptance by forgiving yourself first and everyone in your past.

Commit to learning and finding the resources needed for the talents you want to build or the knowledge you will need for obtaining any goal. Be thankful for all you have every day. Learn to give back to the community or commit acts of kindness. When you receive money always pay yourself first by saving 10-20 percent of everything you make. You may need an emergency fund and some to pay your taxes. But 10Percent must be in a savings for a retirement account such as a stock dividend or an IRA or 401K. When you start saving money and never spend it you will feel powerful and gain confidence Talk to a Financial Planner or advisor. Helping others along the way is a pleasant way to show gratitude. Donate your time or money to a charitable organization or create act of kindness. It always comes back to you 10 fold. Keep a journal and write down positive actions for yourself and those you care about. Always include your loved ones that support you and care about you. When you write down at least 3 good things about yourself every day or every week will create happiness and reasons to be happy. Read inspirational books and self-help books. Read passages everyday 10-15 minutes upon arising and write down your goals for the next day upon retiring. Remember to write the good stuff about yourself as well. Sometimes read before you fall asleep 10-15 minutes. Make it a goal to do every day.

Sometimes fate will change a plan or goal or dream. Be flexible to work through the bumps that interfere. Sometimes People come into your life for a reason. You do not know at the moment what fate will lead you to. Trust in yourself. Believe in yourself. Be Strong enough to know the good choices and the good people from the bad. We all have intuitions that lead us to good things if we allow it. Always be ware of who you are and your weaknesses, so you do not fall into a trap that leads you down the wrong path away from your family and your goals. Learn to make lemonade out of the lemons that come along. Make a path around any hole in the road. Yes there are bumps in the road, just go slow as not to fall in the wholes or traps that lead you away from your plans. Remember to always choose to be happy, no matter what happens. Never quit and never give up. Life is too short to go backwards or get depressed. We are all Angels for each other. Do take a chance to say hello to a stranger or help one another it may lead to amazing journey's you never dreamed of. Accept the challenges along the way to better yourself every day. The pleasures of fate or spirituality may make you laugh or cry with joy. These treasured pleasures will strengthen your mind and soul with spiritually and make you stronger. Your life will flourish into a butterfly and you will grow stronger and happier.

Learn to eat right and be healthy. Always look for ways to improve your diet and health habits. Get into a healthy workout routine and keep smiling. Yoga is one of the best to combine with any routine. Yoga is breath and with good breathing habits gives the body oxygen the livelihood of life. Without breath there is no life. Enjoy the outdoors! Appreciate the flowers, birds and bees. Without bees there would be no food. Because the bees pollinate the food we eat.

Use that google again to research some things that make you healthier and stronger. Maybe even go to a holistic herb doctor to test your blood and give you some knowledgeable guidance for your health. Doctors sometimes over medicate and make you ill or get you on opioids and you end up in an addiction you never planned. The FDA has approved some medicines that kill you and the vaccines are poison I never trusted doctors after I broke my back and a neuro-surgeon put me on demurral shots and I became addicted to them. He then had to send me to a psychiatrist to give me Trazadone to get me off the demurral. It made me a zombie and since then I learned to only trust Chiropractors and holistic herb doctors for my health. Now I am not saying do not go to doctors because there are some needs to go to a doctor. I still use a doctor to get checkups. You need to have your own set of guidelines when it comes to your health. You should know your body better than your doctor, but he may be the only one who can send you to a specialist for more evaluations that he has no control over. I still use google or a search engine of some sort to diagnose or better understand what is wrong with me. But that is me. You have to make your own decisions how to make your life healthy and happy. It is always a great idea to get a second opinion.

Always be aware of your surroundings and surround yourself with people that love you and care about you. Be aware of the clubs you go to and the neighborhoods that are dangerous to always have your armor of love and god around you to protect you. Be aware of the dangers of drugs and gangs and traps that could harm you and or your loved ones that are with you. Don't forget to pray and be thankful kind and considerate to lead them or not let them lead you into danger as well. Guard yourself and your loved ones from alcohol and drugs or sex trafficking ventures. Your intuition as well as guidance from above can save you. Don't be afraid to go to a movie, play or music festival that you choose. Just know that there are dangers of drugs, alcohol and predators that may spoil a venture. Read and sing and dance to your hearts delight or ski, skate or play ball whatever your talents are, choose the ones that benefit your lifestyle and your partners or relations that you are in with.

Learn to love what you hate and you will have no fears you will be fearless and fierce.

Enjoy life's tribulations and graduate to succeed your goals and dreams. Inspire others to grow with you. You will pay a price for your tribulations in life are willing to grow with discipline and self-motivation. There are two of you and always there are more than two choices to make. It takes a window to your soul to make the right choice. If you make the wrong choice you may not be able to correct it so due diligence and time of need or patience is required for either uphill or downhills or crossroads. Be mindful of your surrounding relationships before you choose. There are no mistakes in life only onwards and upwards are the key.

Stay positive and choose only happiness! Not selfishness or negative choices that turn you upside down. Life is a journey of lifelong situations that control or surround your patterns of behavior. Make them fit into your lifestyle for committing to learn and read ethically to enjoy and prosper along the way. You are an amazing being and there is only one of you to share precious moments in life with great and wonderful blessings to behold. You are here for a reason and only you and your creator can make it happen by the choices you make and the decision through trial error you get back up. Never quit and never give up on you. Make it a great life for your partners too. Whenever you get down in life, find someone or something that inspires you to help others along the way. Maybe visit a children's hospital or donate time to the elderly or visit someone else in need so you forget about your problems and take a break. Take a friend on a road trip a or a restaurant that they choose. When you are helping others you forget about your problems and focus on their needs for a change. That gives you time when you do get back to your situation and how to correct it and make it a positive move in the right direction that makes you happy again. Maybe go work out or meditate to create that passion again. Give yourself a break when you need it. Take time to yourself to be kind and thoughtful. Reach beyond your passion with knowledge wisdom courage and strength to be at peace and joy to love everything surrounding you. Enjoy the air, sunlight, rain and everything that has been put on this earth for the betterment of life. Enjoy life and fulfill your passions and dreams with the goals and plans you direct. You are the movie of your life and you are the director and stage manager. Go beyond the movie and you are the script writer. Your life in a movie will be the best movie ever played out in real life. You get to pick the actors and actresses and places you desire your life to be in. Make it full of loving and giving and passion without drama and violence. Imagine that! Would it be boring? You may have some violence and drama along the way because in reality we all have a daily movie and the action make it exciting and fun. Since you are the star and everything else in the movie that you are directing… you need to be the hero. So as you write and direct you will run into drama… just make it end with nice lemonade and be the hero you want to be in life. Figure out how to win the challenges that you are faced with. Go write and direct your movie with challenges and inspiration. Add the drama and plots to save you from danger and disasters. In reality, isn't life just a game? It all depends on who the players are and everyone has a motive that gives us the challenges that we face in real life. You can be far ahead of the game by knowing the rules to get around the plots and schemes in everyday scenarios.

Who knows it might even hit the Big Cinema Screens and be an Oscar winner.

You may have to take risks to gain whatever you are trying to achieve. Be persistent and patient. There is no crystal ball that says anything is right or wrong. It is choices that give you crossroads and hill to climb. Stay on track with your dreams and goals to face your fears and overcome them. There are no failures only bumps in the road that you may have to dodge. Take action to be aware of dangers and stay positive and happy at all times. Develop communication skills to overcome self-pity and low self-esteem. In fact, let those terms not be a part of your life. Stay Strong. Spend time with your family get to know what they want and help them as well as helping yourself.

Give yourself the gift of love and friendship to mirror your desired inspirational being that you will or have become. Be the friend you always wanted in your life. Model yourself with passion and desire to become the person you dream of being. You are a child of God or your creator, special in his presents. Be the rock of armor that protects you from all deviations underneath that may crawl out and sneak upon you. Stay in a long lasting relationship with your loved ones and keep on praying and thanking your creator every day for all you have and are to become let it be in his glory to Him we pray Amen. Go relentlessly with the gifts of pleasure and pride with the power and the strength you will acquire with Him always by your side to never stray. Look in the mirror as a window to your soul to reach beyond your imagination to become Fearless and Fierce!

I AM REQUESTING REVIEWS. You can email me at aandrsn@ hotmail.com

Printed in the United States
By Bookmasters